Using Formative Assessment
to Improve Student Outcomes in Classrooms

MICHAEL W. CONNELL

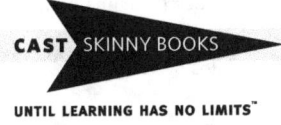

Bulk discounts available: For details, email publishing@cast.org or visit www.castpublishing.org.

Copyright © 2020 by CAST, Inc. All rights reserved.

No part of this publication may be reproduced or transmitted in any form or by any means, electronic or mechanical, including photocopy, recording, or any information storage and retrieval systems, without permission in writing from the publisher.

Library of Congress Control Number: 2019949824

Paperback ISBN 978-1-930583-04-7
Ebook ISBN 978-1-930583-22-1

Published by:
CAST Professional Publishing
an imprint of CAST, Inc.
Wakefield, Massachusetts, USA

SKINNY BOOKS® is a registered trademark of CAST, Inc.
Cover and interior design by Happenstance Type-O-Rama
Cover image by © Sutterstock | one line man

Printed in the United States of America

"Things won't go perfect. It's all about how you adapt from those things and learn from mistakes."
—MICHAEL PHELPS, OLYMPIC SWIMMER WITH A RECORD 23 GOLD MEDALS

Contents

About the Author vii

Introduction ix

1 Individualized Instruction Is Central to All Great Teaching 1
Key Takeaways 10

2 Why Should Teachers Care about Formative Assessment? 11
Why Is Formative Assessment Necessary? 15
Formative Assessment—Perhaps the Most Powerful Teaching Tool We Know 21
Key Takeaways 24

3 Components of Formative Assessment in Practice. 25
Example #1: Arithmetic 26
Example #2: Social Studies 28
How Can Classroom Teachers Use Formative Assessment More Effectively? 31
Evaluating Teaching Methods with Respect to Their Use of Formative Assessment 32
Key Takeaways 42

4 Formative Assessment in Some Group Instruction Scenarios **43**
Interactive Lecture 45
The Flipped Classroom 50
Programmed Instruction 55
Adaptive Educational Software 60
Teacher Dashboard. 67
Summary 71
Key Takeaways 74

5 Closing Thoughts **75**
Let's Connect! 77

References **79**

About the Author

Michael W. Connell, Ed.D., is an educational designer, researcher, and consultant. He served on the faculties of Harvard University (in the Graduate School of Education), Dartmouth College (educational neuroscience program), and the University of Texas (Southwest Center for Mind, Brain, and Education). During his career, he worked in many educational environments, from early childhood (as founder and CEO of education technology company Native Brain, Inc.) to K–12 (as research associate and software design engineer in the Advanced Research and Development Lab at Lexia Learning Systems, Inc.) to professional training and development across a variety of industries (including medicine, technology, and teacher professional development). In much of this work, he has successfully used formative assessment as a central design principle to produce engaging and effective differentiated learning experiences that are also scalable.

Mike earned a Bachelor's Degree in Electrical Engineering and a Bachelor's Degree in Computer Science from MIT, with a concentration in brain and cognitive sciences and a particular interest in human and machine learning. He went on to earn a Master of Science in Electrical Engineering and Computer Science from MIT, working in the areas of artificial intelligence and robotics.

Shifting his attention to human learning and education, he received a Master's Degree and a Doctorate in Human Development and Psychology from the Harvard Graduate School of Education, with a concentration in Cognitive Development.

Mike currently leads a team that delivers transformative training and organizational change services to R&D organizations. He enjoys speaking, writing, and teaching about the learning sciences, educational technology, and evidence-based educational design.

Introduction

What comes to mind when you hear the word *assessment*? Many people think of pop quizzes and final exams (maybe with an inner groan)—the dreaded tests of knowledge that teachers often use to determine students' grades in a class.

In reality, though, *assessment* is not a synonym for *test*—the two are different. A test is fundamentally a *measurement* instrument—it simply associates a number with some aspect of a student's performance. That number can be used in different ways. Assessment, in contrast, involves the *interpretation* of a measurement like a test score. This distinction between the test (measure) and assessment (interpretation) is often overlooked, but it is much more important than it might seem on the face of it. In fact, *formative assessment*—the process of interpreting data on student performance to adapt instruction to individual needs—is perhaps the single most powerful tool available to teachers to help every student succeed to their full potential. To understand why, let's move away from the classroom for a moment into a realm where the distinction might be easier to recognize—competitive sports.

Consider Michael Phelps, the Olympic champion swimmer. For competitive swimmers like Phelps, swim time is a key measure of performance (it's like a swimmer's test score). Swim times can be assessed (or interpreted) in different ways, though (see Figure I.1). The swim time is just a number. But if that number (measured in official competition) is lower than the time associated with the current world record, then it becomes the new world record—a very big deal indeed! This is an example of *summative* assessment. Like the final grade in a class, the official competitive swim time represents a kind of cumulative (or summary) evaluation reflecting the result of a substantial period of learning and development. In other words, summative assessment is like a snapshot of someone's current competency.

Figure I.1. From one measurement, two different kinds of assessment: formative and summative.

There is a second way to interpret the same measurement, however: *formatively*. During practice, for example, Phelps's coach Bob Bowman would time him. These times were not official times that could be used to rank him or establish world records, but were used to help him identify areas for improvement that would develop greater speed over time. For example, Bowman describes how in the early days of their work together he identified a major flaw in Phelps's butterfly stroke that had to do with his breathing—Phelps would lift his head too far out of the water when taking a breath, and lose precious fractions of a second each time. In this case, the measured swim time becomes diagnostic, revealing that something about the performance needs improvement. Observing the swimmer's technique carefully, the coach identifies an aspect of the performance (breathing) that is wasting time and provides detailed feedback to the student. Over time, with practice and individualized support, the student's performance (swim time) improves, suggesting that the intervention is having the desired effect. Instead of looking backward to take a snapshot of current capability, formative assessment is used in a forward-looking way to adapt the instruction to deliberately shape (or form) the skill toward a specific end. Formative assessment is the secret to producing champion athletes, and it's also the secret to producing successful outcomes for all students in a classroom.

There is a wrinkle, however, in that classroom teachers rarely have the luxury of working with a single student at a time. And anyone who has worked with children knows how wildly diverse they are. Even parents with more than one child often comment—with some amazement—on how different their own children are from each other, and how surprised they were to discover this, given that their kids share 50% of the same genes, grew up in the same household, and look alike. Indeed, many people—especially those who have not spent much time with children—seem to assume that children are all pretty similar when it comes to learning and development.

Veteran classroom teachers are under no such illusions. They experience firsthand how widely students of similar age in a single classroom differ in terms of personality, coordination, intelligence, prior knowledge, interests, motivation, temperament, emotional regulation, attention, memory, self-confidence, attitudes about learning, maturity, self-discipline, and so on—all of which influence their learning. Just to take one example in the area of math, it is well documented that some students have mastered at age three what other students are still struggling to learn at age seven and beyond—evidence of an achievement gap of at least *four years* right at the beginning of formal schooling. And this massive diversity in capabilities and needs is what gives rise to what may be the grand challenge of teaching—how to help every child in such a diverse group succeed.

I remember discussing this with a friend. He and his family live in a district with some of the best public schools in their state. And yet they were disappointed that their two girls did not seem to be learning at anywhere near their full potential. Frustrated, he and his wife decided to pull the children out of public school and homeschool them. Under this arrangement, he reported that both kids were able to advance four academic grade levels in two calendar years. My friend took this as confirmation that the schools were underperforming. "If my wife can produce these outcomes *without even having any special teacher training,*" he reasoned, "then shouldn't public school teachers with all of their training and experience be able to do at least this well for my children?"

At that moment I had a flash of insight—he was making an apples-to-oranges comparison between the homeschool scenario and the public school scenario, imagining that the only relevant difference in the two situations was the teacher. "What would happen," I asked him, "if your wife tried to teach your children along with 25 others in a public school classroom? Do you think she'd still be able to achieve the results you saw at home?" The answer is obviously "no." The reality is that outcomes of one-on-one instruction are simply not comparable to outcomes of group instruction. A teacher's skill in instructing individual students is obviously important, but that has historically not been as much of a factor in classroom teaching as being able to manage and instruct a large group of students.

 A CLOSER LOOK Sadler (1998) defines formative assessment as "specifically intended to provide feedback on performance to improve and accelerate learning." See https://bit.ly/2ZsCr6Q for Sadler's article.

My friend's story does highlight an important issue, though. The fact is that virtually all students—like his daughters—are capable of learning much more with individualized instruction than they typically could in a group setting. And teachers know they could teach any given student more effectively one-on-one than they can in a group. The difference in outcomes is quite striking, in fact. Research stretching back decades has documented, for example, that one-on-one instruction can move the average student to the top of the class—above 98% of the students who are taught with traditional methods of group instruction such as lectures and worksheets (Bloom, 1984).

Hearing this, many people—like my friend—might wonder, "If students are capable of learning so much more, and teachers are capable of teaching so much more, then why isn't that happening?" The core challenge has to do with scale—with one teacher to 20 or 30 students, the one-on-one model breaks down and teachers have to start making hard choices about how to allocate their limited time and attention. For example, sometimes they have to choose between moving quickly through the curriculum and leaving some students behind, or moving slowly to accommodate the trailing students at the cost of holding the more advanced students back and possibly falling behind schedule.

PAUSE AND THINK Think about a time when you saw a look of confusion on a student's face. What did you do? You might have taken a moment to ask some probing questions in order to identify the specific source of their confusion or misunderstanding. That's one example of an informal formative assessment. Formative assessment also can be done formally by using a test specifically designed for that purpose, for example. Skilled teachers use assessments like this all the time.

The question we tackle in this book is the following: what makes one-on-one instruction so much more effective than group instruction, and how can we use that understanding to make group teaching more effective? The short answer is by using formative assessment to customize instruction. In the following sections we begin with an overview of formative assessment—what it is and how it works. Next, we develop a simple framework to help us understand how formative assessment is incorporated into different teaching methods. Finally, we use the framework to explore some specific methods that can enable teachers to use formative assessment more effectively in their classrooms.

More specifically, in this book I will show that

- You already know what formative assessment is and some ways to use it in your classroom teaching.

- Understanding how to use formative assessment more effectively will improve your practice.

- Some relatively straightforward methods can help every teacher apply formative assessment more effectively with a group.

- More sophisticated methods of formative assessment in the classroom require more work but can produce even bigger gains in student achievement for those who are willing and able to apply them.

Key Takeaways

- Individualized instruction—bridging between the generic curriculum and individual student capabilities and needs—is at the heart of all good teaching.
- Formative assessment is a key to success in school and in life because it enables us to improve while there is still opportunity to do so.

1

Individualized Instruction Is Central to All Great Teaching

It is well-established—and probably will not surprise many teachers—that students can learn much more through one-on-one instruction than they typically do through traditional group teaching methods in a classroom. The question is, why? And how can we teach in a group as effectively as one-on-one? Let's explore these questions by considering some unrealistically extreme—but nonetheless informative—teaching scenarios.

Imagine a class of 25 students who have a one-hour period for math instruction during a school day. Let's say (perhaps optimistically) it takes 10 minutes to transition from the previous activity (get set up, get everyone settled, and so on), leaving 50 minutes of learning time available in the math period. How might the teacher use that time?

At one extreme, the teacher might think about applying the one-on-one instructional model directly. She might, for example, work with each student one-on-one as much as possible. Dividing the 50-minute teaching period equally among 25 students means she could walk from desk to desk spending two minutes with each student providing individualized instruction, while the others wait patiently. This strategy is clearly not reasonable in reality, but contemplating it can help to surface some of the challenges that arise in a group setting but not in a one-on-one interaction, including

- This method is terribly ineffective, in that two minutes of instructional time is woefully insufficient to individualize teaching—it could easily take more than two minutes just to diagnose what a student understands about a single concept, let alone figure out what he or she needs and how best to support him or her.
- In addition, this method would be terribly inefficient in terms of how it uses precious teacher time, since there would be a lot of repetition as the teacher tries to introduce the same set of concepts to each student individually.
- This strategy is also terribly inefficient from the student's perspective, since it would result in a huge waste of potential learning time for the students, as they sit idle for 48 minutes waiting for their two minutes of instruction. Also, with two minutes of instruction per hour, the teacher would not be able to cover much material at all with any student.

At the other extreme, a teacher might spend the whole 50 minutes delivering the same prepared lecture to the whole class that she delivers every year, with no time for questions and no individualized attention. This strategy actually appears to be substantially better than the previous scenario (where there were two minutes of individualized instruction per student):

- It is a more efficient use of student learning time, since students are all engaged in—or at least exposed to—a learning activity for the full 50 minutes.
- It is less redundant from a teaching standpoint, since all students receive the same instruction, delivered once.
- It is probably more effective, in that—all else equal—it seems plausible that more learning can generally be accomplished with 50 minutes of lecture than with two minutes of individual instruction. At least there could be a reasonable amount of coverage of the subject matter.

But what's missing from this second scenario? The actual teaching! That is, the teacher has no opportunity to interact with the students and apply her teaching expertise to enhance individual student learning. To understand what this means, just consider that in this extreme scenario where there is literally zero teacher-student interaction, a prepared live lecture would be virtually equivalent to having the students watch a pre-recorded video for the entire period. And if the live teacher could be replaced with a video series with comparable outcomes, then that teacher would seem to be engaged in a form of broadcasting information, not teaching.

As these scenarios make clear, the reason lecture and video are such common group instruction methods is not because they are more effective than individualized instruction but because of the practical logistical difficulties associated with individualizing instruction when working with a group of students. Differentiating instruction effectively in a group setting, in other words, requires a shift in mindset and in practice as to what good teaching looks like.

Reflecting on these two extreme scenarios, we might compare them to each other and to one-on-one instruction to ask, what does a teacher add to the educational enterprise that is unique? You might say that teachers *explain things*. That is true. But books explain things, too—so why can't students just read books? You might say reading requires more skill and effort than listening, and that generally seems to be true. So why not let students listen to audio books or watch videos on YouTube? You should be furrowing your brow right now if you thought "teachers explain things" was a good answer to the question—it's true, but it seems insufficient, doesn't it?

Let's try refining the question: What does a competent teacher do live that goes beyond what students could get from reading a book or watching a video on their own? First, learning is hard work and, left to their own devices, many children (and adults!) would prefer to engage in entertainment or some other activity rather than education—playing games instead of reading about World War II, for example, or watching cartoons in lieu of watching a video about long division.

Clearly, one important responsibility teachers have is to monitor the room and ensure every student is engaged with the current learning activity, whatever form it takes. For some students, it may be enough for the teacher simply to redirect their attention to the activity periodically. Some students may need help figuring out how to organize their efforts to do the work—what steps to take, what to do first, and so on. In other cases, students may need to be moved or separated from friends. Some students need to be engaged motivationally; for instance, by "catching their interest" somehow.

 A CLOSER LOOK For more on classroom management, check out this APA teacher module at https://bit.ly/2dlYscy.

Here we can actually see two important responsibilities that teachers perform that books and videos cannot—they scaffold students' management of their own strategic mental resources (like attention and executive function) and they provide motivational coaching. Note that these teaching responsibilities can both be handled at the group level—by designing a widely appealing activity, for example—or at the individual level, such as by intervening with an individual student when it is clear they are not doing the work.

Drilling deeper, we might ask what causes students to disengage in the first place. There are many possible reasons. Students might have an attention or executive function disability. They might be hungry, tired, too hot, or too cold. They might be uncomfortable sitting in the chair for long periods of time. Students might be distracted by something more interesting than the work presented to them, such as social interaction, doodling, or (these days) consuming media or playing games on a digital device. Teachers may be able to address some of these issues, while others may be beyond their control. Any or all of these factors can create disruptions that steal precious time from learning and teaching activities.

Students also commonly disengage because the work is not at their "just right level." Specifically, the work may be too difficult, which will make students act out in frustration, or the work may be too easy, which will make them tune out from boredom when their minds wander to something more interesting.

Note that motivation is not generally controllable through an act of sheer will. Think for a moment: Have you ever tried forcing yourself to learn something you weren't interested in learning, or to do something difficult that you didn't want to do, or to do something really boring for an extended period of time? Have you ever found yourself reading and rereading the same passage in a book several times, unable to understand what it says because it was particularly dense or because you were distracted by something else at the time? If you answered "yes" to any of these questions, then you know from personal experience that motivation is not simply a matter of exerting your will, or "applying yourself" to get it done. The conditions and context have a huge effect on your ability to become engaged and stay engaged. Moreover, younger people on the whole are even less well-equipped than adults to manage their own motivation, since both their skills and their nervous systems are less developed. Finally, students—like all people—vary biologically and psychologically in their motivational makeup. This means that some students have an easier time than others staying engaged with learning for reasons that may be beyond their control.

The academic challenge students face must also be well-matched to their capabilities and needs—not just in a general sense, as in "they are ready for third grade." It must be matched in a very specific and nuanced sense, as in "this student doesn't understand the concept of place value" or "this student doesn't have the vocabulary to comprehend this chapter book." A book or a video can neither diagnose these individual issues nor respond to them and bridge the specific gap in understanding experienced by an individual student.

> **A CLOSER LOOK** Most educators are familiar with Carol Dweck's groundbreaking work on growth mindset. Watch her TED Talk "The Power of Believing that You Can Improve" at https://bit.ly/1sGo5O0.

Here we see a third crucial function live teachers perform that books and videos cannot: Teachers bridge the gap between the curriculum as-it-is and the curriculum as it is experienced by a student, given their unique capabilities and needs. If that gap is too large, a student becomes frustrated, and the teacher can find ways to make the challenge more reasonable. If the gap is too small—the student already knows the material well, for example—then the teacher can find ways to make it more challenging so the student does not get bored.

> **A CLOSER LOOK** The Universal Design for Learning (UDL) Guidelines offer helpful suggestions on how to increase student engagement. See http://udlguidelines.cast.org/engagement.

To summarize, in the foregoing discussion we identified the unique value and essence of live teaching, which is the teacher's ability to bridge between what the generic curriculum demands and what each individual student is capable of accomplishing successfully. In other words, *individualizing* the generic curriculum for each student is the essence of live instruction that makes it more effective than self-study through books and videos. We identified three different dimensions along which teachers adapt or individualize the curriculum for students:

1. *Strategic (or metacognitive) scaffolding*: A teacher helps each student manage their attention, get organized to do the work, prioritize, manage time and materials, set goals, evaluate their own performance, and so on.
2. *Motivational coaching*: A teacher finds ways to keep students engaged in the work and on task, motivated to persist and learn, and confident in their ability to succeed at the tasks set for them.
3. *Individualizing learning challenge*: Students vary widely in their prior knowledge and learning capabilities. If a task is beyond their capability, they will fail at it. Repeated failure can erode confidence and self-image as a capable learner. If a task is too easy, they will learn little or nothing, and more importantly, they will become bored and easily distracted. Repeated and extended boredom can erode interest in learning generally and create an aversion to school specifically. Individualizing a learning task to match the specific capabilities and needs of an individual student requires evaluating the challenge mismatch (for example, too easy or too hard), diagnosing the cause (for example,

the student has already mastered fractions or the student does not have the necessary background vocabulary), and adapting the challenge appropriately (for instance, providing a hint or example if the challenge is too great, or suggesting avenues for deeper exploration if the challenge is insufficient).

This conclusion—that the essence of effective instruction is in finding ways to bridge between the generic curriculum and individual student capabilities and needs—is borne out by the research literature on one-on-one tutoring. In particular, Bloom (1984) found that the average student with one-on-one tutoring could perform at the level of the best students (top two percent) in typical group instruction. It would seem there is potential for improvement when it comes to group classroom teaching—and perhaps that improvement is within our reach.

Key Takeaways

- One-on-one instruction allows the teacher to adapt instruction to the needs of an individual, which is often quite intuitive for teachers and very effective for students.
- The tactics that work so well one-on-one break down in group settings, leading teachers to fall back on non-individualized methods such as lectures.
- Thinking productively about individualizing instruction when in a group therefore requires a shift in mindset and in practice.

2

Why Should Teachers Care about Formative Assessment?

What does any of this have to do with formative assessment? This may seem a bit confusing at first, but what we have identified as the essence of effective teaching—the teacher's ability to bridge from the generic curriculum to an individual student's needs—*is* formative assessment. One source of confusion is the name itself: *formative assessment*. It's really a technical term. Many people using the word informally treat the word *assessment* as if it is a synonym for *test* or *exam*. As we discussed briefly in the introduction, that's incorrect.

A test is a measurement instrument—like a ruler or a thermometer. Formative assessment is actually a *process*. It is the process of using individual student data—whether informal as in a teacher's observation of a student's look of confusion, or formal as in a score on a unit quiz—to adjust instruction in a responsive way, or to individualize it. The appropriate adjustment will of course differ for individual students.

Let's return to the example of Olympian Michael Phelps. When he practices for an event before the Olympics, his coach measures his time using a stopwatch. During an Olympic event, the officials also measure his time with a stopwatch. His measured time in both cases is the same kind of measurement (swim time) using the same kind of measurement instrument (stopwatch). The time measurement is like an exam in school—it's simply a measurement that associates a number with some aspect of a performance we care about.

Neither raw measure—the swim time nor the exam score—is an assessment. Assessment is the process of *interpreting* the measures. Note that unlike a measurement, context is required to make an assessment, in that raw measures have to be interpreted against some standard. There are two ways to interpret a measure: a summative assessment and a formative assessment.

Summative assessment is the process of evaluating students' learning at the end of an instructional unit using learning goals, standards, and other benchmarks to gauge how well they did in relation to the unit's objectives. Returning to the Olympic example, when Michael Phelps competes in an official Olympic event, his time is measured along with all of the other swimmers' times. The times are rank-ordered, with the fastest time awarded the gold medal (first place), the second fastest time awarded the silver medal, and the third fastest time awarded the bronze medal. The other swimmers' times provide the benchmarks against which the quality of a performance is evaluated at the end of an event. This is a summative assessment because of the way the data are used—to determine the rank ordering of performances and designate final winners. In a classroom, a student's final grade is perhaps the best example of a summative assessment—it provides a final evaluation summarizing the quality of their attainment in relation to learning objectives, standards, and other benchmarks over the course of the whole semester or year. The final grade cannot by its very nature be used to adapt instruction for a student, though—the period of instruction is over.

Formative assessment is the process of evaluating student learning as it occurs, with the express purpose of using the data to identify ways to adapt teaching and learning methods to increase student achievement. For example, when Michael Phelps practices before the Olympics, his coach measures his swim time. This measurement is exactly the same kind used in the Olympic events, but the measurement is used for a different assessment. The assessment is not summative—that is, "you won" or "you lost" or "you came in third"—instead, the assessment is used to diagnose and provide specific feedback so Phelps can improve his performance in the next run. Observing Phelps's form and his time at the end of a run, for instance, his coach might tell him, "that was your worst time today—you lost time at the start; try a flatter angle at the launch" or "your times have been consistently better since you changed the way you are handling turns—let's keep doing that and see if we can smooth out the stroke rate now." There may still be an evaluation against a standard, as there is in these examples, but the key difference is that such an evaluation is then used to inform how to adapt behavior to improve outcomes in the next iteration.

The "gold star" idea here is that the measurement—whether it is a swim time measured with a stopwatch or math performance measured with a pop quiz—is not an assessment. The type of test does not determine the type of assessment. The type of assessment is determined by *how the measured data are used to evaluate performance.* You might think of a test as a *tool,* summative assessment as a *product,* and formative assessment as an ongoing *process.* The figure from the introduction is worth considering again here:

Measurement/Test:
Assigns a value to some aspect of performance

Formative Assessment:
Process of using data to adapt instruction.

Summative Assessment:
Interpretation of data to provide a snapshot of current competency.

Why Is Formative Assessment Necessary?

If the human brain were like a movie camera, then we could in theory turn it on, present the information we want students to learn, and turn it off, and the information would be stored perfectly, just the way it was presented. Unfortunately, the human brain works nothing like a movie camera. In fact, there is no such thing as "one-trial learning" for human beings, which is essentially what a recording device does. Instead, all knowledge is constructed progressively over time. Even if we could instantly memorize what we see and hear, like a recording device, that would not actually solve our problem. That information would be stored entirely in one kind of memory system, called "declarative memory." It would not be usable; learning is a constructive process, not a recording process.

To become usable knowledge, the information has to be integrated with a variety of memory systems and it has to be assimilated to other knowledge we already have. This process of taking in new information through our eyes and ears and other senses and constructing new knowledge out of it is a slow process that is also prone to misunderstanding and other kinds of errors. It never happens in a single instance—even though it sometimes seems that way, such as when a person "suddenly" comes to understand something. The understanding may have "clicked" in an instant, but the person never learns everything that is relevant to that understanding in an instant. At the very least, that new understanding is building on a great deal of prior knowledge developed over years or decades.

The process of knowledge construction is also not directly visible to us (as students, teachers, or observers). When students encounter new information, we do not immediately know what they will retain (if anything) or what meaning they will make of it—in particular, whether they will take away an accurate understanding, a wild misconception, or something in between. In fact, every student experiences a unique learning process based on their prior knowledge, learning capacity, interest, attentional control, and so on and internalizes the "same" information presented by a teacher in a different way.

As a result, if we want to ensure that students are actually learning what is intended, we need a way to monitor learning continuously as we develop the target knowledge. Typically, this means we introduce a new concept or skill, we have the student work with it and relate it to other knowledge somehow (through exercises, projects, writing about connections to other concepts and skills, and so on), we measure their understanding, we diagnose any gaps or misconceptions, and we address them by adapting the instruction in some way (intervention). The tighter the formative assessment loop, the better. That is, the more student learning can be monitored and the more the teacher's instruction can be adapted to ensure and enhance student learning (Figure 2.1), the more optimal the formative assessment.

The formative assessment process is not something new. In fact, teachers everywhere already use it on a daily basis. If a student raises her hand to ask a question and the teacher answers it, that is an example of formative assessment. If a science teacher gives a pop quiz on Friday and adjusts his teaching on the nervous system

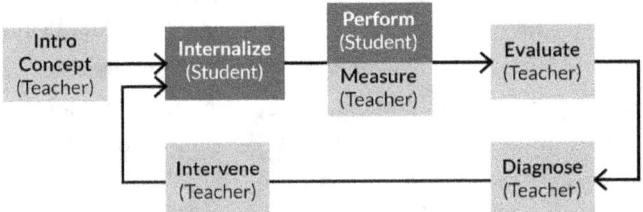

Figure 2.1: The typical process of adapting instruction using formative assessment in a one-on-one teaching scenario.

as a result, that is a formative assessment. If a teacher notices a student looks confused or upset, reviews their work, asks some probing questions, and suggests ways to improve understanding, that is formative assessment. In every case the teacher collects data (formally or informally), interprets the data, decides on a course of action, and changes instruction to improve student learning.

Formative assessment is the process of bridging the generic curriculum to individual learning needs. More specifically, formative assessment is the process of using data to decide how to modify a learning task to better match a student's "just right" level. Formative assessment is typically defined primarily as "individualizing the learning challenge," focusing less on the other two dimensions of effective live instruction identified earlier: strategic scaffolding and motivational coaching. This may be because teachers are often able to diagnose problems in these other two areas pretty readily and have general strategies for responding, at least to the surface symptoms.

If a child is staring out the window when he is supposed to be doing a math worksheet, for example, the teacher can plainly see that he is disengaged. The teacher can quickly scan the student's progress up to that point to see if he understands the task and re-explain the instructions if not (strategic scaffolding), or gently remind the student to attend to the work (motivational coaching) and move on. These actions—which are administered individually but do not necessarily require a great deal of nuanced insight about the student's mental state—may be effective in some cases.

However, in cases where the disconnect is deeper and grounded in a mismatch between the demands of the activity and the capabilities of the student—such as when a student doesn't have the background vocabulary to make sense of a book chapter that has been assigned—then strategic scaffolding and motivational coaching will generally be insufficient to facilitate learning. Note that making the challenge appropriate for each child should have secondary benefits in these other two areas as well (Brookhart, 2010). In particular, if a challenge is well-matched to capabilities, the chances of boredom and frustration decrease, making it easier for students to stay engaged, motivated, and focused on the learning task, and decreasing the incidence of behavioral outbursts that may disrupt others in the class.

A major challenge is that there is no obvious way for a teacher to tell what the root cause of the student's problem is by simply looking at him or her. This is why measurement (tests, quizzes, oral reports, worked problems, and other observable performances of understanding) are necessary—to make the learning visible. This way, a teacher can 1) assess the student's need, and 2) decide the best way to support their learning—in the same way that Michael Phelps's coach uses measured swim times plus other observations of his performance to help Phelps improve steadily over time.

Let's return to the two extreme teaching scenarios introduced earlier. On one extreme we had the scenario where the 50-minute math period was divided equally into two-minute segments that the teacher would spend individually with each student. At the other extreme was the 50-minute "canned lecture" with zero teacher-student interaction (see Figure 2.2).

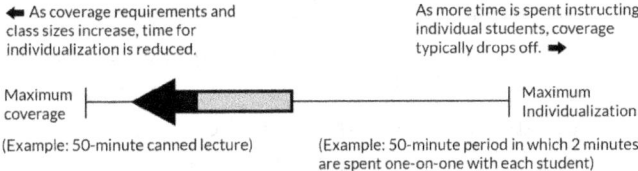

Figure 2.2: The tradeoff between coverage and individualization in group instruction.

In one-on-one tutoring, with one teacher and one student, all of the teacher's time can be spent individualizing instruction for that one student, without sacrificing time spent on coverage. As soon as there is more than one student, however, the classroom teacher is faced with a dilemma—a tradeoff between coverage on the one hand and individualization on the other, and the tension grows more acute with each additional student. At the extreme, for example, she could maximize coverage by sacrificing all individualization with a 50-minute lecture, or she could maximize individualization while dramatically sacrificing coverage by spending two minutes on one-on-one instruction with each of her 25 students in the same 50-minute period.

Most teachers typically operate somewhere between these extremes. For example, they might spend half the time giving the students whole-group instruction or having them watch an instructional video and then spend the other half of the time individualizing—answering questions and walking the room to check in on individual student progress on a worksheet or other activity and providing support where necessary. Given the requirement to cover a certain amount of content within the fixed time available in the school year, there is often pressure for teachers to operate closer to the left side of the continuum in Figure 2.2—spending the bulk of class time on coverage activities (lectures, videos, and so on) and leaving less time for individualization. And as coverage and class size increase, there is pressure to shift the balance progressively further toward coverage at the expense of individualization through formative assessment. This trend is unfortunately in the wrong direction given that *more* formative assessment (or data-driven individualization) is associated with *better* student outcomes.

 PAUSE AND THINK In many classrooms, the balance between coverage and individualization is closer to the coverage side, and as coverage requirements—and class sizes—increase, the balance tends to move progressively further in that direction.

Where do you fall on this continuum? In other words, how much time do you typically spend presenting a fixed curriculum versus using data on student understanding to adapt instruction to individual student needs? What factors affect this balance in your experience?

Formative Assessment—Perhaps the Most Powerful Teaching Tool We Know

If teachers are already using formative assessment to some degree in their classroom teaching (you might ask) then why do we need a book on the subject? Good question.

The reason is that there is a big difference between what we might call *ad hoc* formative assessment and *designed* formative assessment. In fact, it is more of a continuum than two distinct categories.

Formative assessment is more *ad hoc* to the degree that it uses informal observations and general probes to diagnose a student's need, and uses general or ad hoc tactics to intervene with the student on the fly. Examples include

- A teacher gives a lecture, a student asks a question, and the teacher answers it.

- A student is staring out the window, a teacher notices and asks the student what's wrong, the student says she doesn't understand what she is meant to do, and the teacher explains the instructions again.

- The class is completing a multiplication worksheet. The teacher walks the room and notices that one student is making much slower progress than most of the others, so the teacher examines his work and discovers that the student does not seem to understand the multiplication procedure. The teacher works through a few examples slowly to help the student grasp the key idea.

These are all perfectly fine examples of formative assessment. But notice that in each case the teacher is basically dividing up the instructional time to work one-on-one with individual students, which as we noted before is limited by the average amount of instructional time available per student. Also, the teacher is reacting to whatever issue comes to her attention, which may or may not be the most important issue to address at that moment, instead of systematically and intentionally designing formative assessment into the instruction to surface and prioritize a wider range of student issues.

At the other end of the continuum, formative assessment is more *designed* to the degree that it uses formal measurement (like a carefully constructed test) or individualized probes to gather diagnostic data about gaps in all students' understanding and uses highly targeted interventions that match very specific student needs. Following are some examples.

Teachers assess student reading levels at the beginning of the year, select books appropriate to their reading level, and then have volunteer parents spend time each week reading with each student, assessing periodically to decide when to increase the challenge level.

A science teacher implements a mastery learning system in which students pull a leveled activity card from a box, complete the activity, and check their own work against the solution on the back of the card. They continue working at their current level until they meet a certain criterion (e.g., completing three cards in a row correctly at the current level) and then they move up to the next level. The teacher walks around providing individual help.

Students work on a math curriculum at their own pace using an adaptive iPad app that simultaneously feeds the student progress data to a dashboard that the teacher can scan to see who is racing ahead and who is struggling.

This gives the teacher immediate insight into what specific concepts and skills are giving them trouble, and the teacher can therefore see every student's progress at every moment, prioritize student issues, and intervene where it will have the greatest benefit for the class.

According to researchers, formative assessment is perhaps the most powerful educational intervention that is known (Black & William, 1998). As stated previously, formative assessment used optimally can take a student who is performing at the average level in a classroom using traditional methods and put them near the top of that class, while also reducing achievement gaps across the group. To put this in context, if the United States could use formative assessment effectively at scale, it could take the entire country from its place in the middle of the pack on international exams like the PISA or TIMSS to just behind the top-performing Pacific Rim countries (Black & William, 1998). Gains of this magnitude in student outcomes, however, are not typically associated with the kinds of ad hoc formative assessment that teachers use spontaneously and intuitively. Such gains have generally been documented where teachers take the more systematic approach to explicitly designing formative assessment into their teaching.

Key Takeaways

- Tests and assessments are different—a test is a *measurement* of some aspect of performance whereas an assessment involves an *interpretation* of some measurement in relation to some standard.

- A summative assessment is like a summary or snapshot of a student's current level of capability in a particular area of knowledge or skill.

- Formative assessment is the process of using data to modify a learning task to better match a student's "just right" level.

- Figuring out how to successfully incorporate more designed formative assessment into their classroom instruction may be the most powerful lever available to teachers who seek to improve student outcomes and reduce achievement gaps.

3

Components of Formative Assessment in Practice

In this chapter, let's consider what actually goes into creating effective formative assessments. The best way of accomplishing this is by looking at real examples. In Chapter 4, we will see how this plays out in a variety of group scenarios.

Sadler defines formative assessment as "assessment that is specifically intended to provide feedback on performance to improve and accelerate learning" (Sadler, 1998, p. 77). Elsewhere, he explains that "formative assessment is concerned with how the patterns and quality of student responses (performances, pieces, or works) can be used to shape and improve the student's competence by short circuiting the randomness and inefficiency of trial-and-error learning" (Sadler, 1989, p. 120). Elawar and Corno (1985) operationalized the process of formative assessment more specifically with a few questions teachers should ask themselves in response to a student error:

- What is the key error? (measurement and evaluation)

- What is the probable reason the student made this error? (diagnosis)
- How can I guide the student to avoid this error in the future? (intervention)

Building on these principles, we can say that a good formative assessment question is specifically designed to serve two purposes:

1. It reliably distinguishes between students who do and do not understand the target concept or skill, which is what enables the teacher to *evaluate* whether the student or group is ready to move on to the next topic.
2. Wrong answers are designed to provide the teacher with *diagnostic insight* about the most important student misconceptions, which is what enables the teacher to determine what specific kind of instructional adaptation is appropriate.

Let's look at a few specific examples from different subject areas.

Example #1: Arithmetic

In an arithmetic class, imagine a student works a long addition problem like this:

```
  567
+ 345
-----
  802
```

The answer should be 912, of course. We can run through Elawar and Corno's three questions above:

What is the key error? The student has carried out the long addition incorrectly. Specifically, he has failed to carry the 1 when the sum in a column is greater than 10. However, notice that he has calculated the one's place correctly in each column. For example, in the right-hand column, 7+5=12, he wrote down the 2 correctly, but failed to carry the extra 10 to the next column. Similarly, in the middle column (ignoring the extra 1 that should have been carried over from the first column), 6+4=10, he wrote down the 0 correctly but failed to carry the extra 1 into the hundreds column.

What is the probable reason the student made this error? There are a few reasons the student might have made this error. The numbers the student wrote down suggest he can carry out small calculations accurately, so addition facts are probably not the root problem in this case. The student also wrote down only one digit per column, which suggests he has at least a basic understanding of place value. Without additional data on the student's performance in this area, the most likely reason for this particular pattern of errors is that the student does not understand conceptually how the place value system relates to the quantities encoded in the numbers, and (possibly as a result of that) does not have fluency in using the long addition procedure when carrying is involved.

How can I guide the student to avoid this error in the future? If the teacher has reason to believe this student understands place value conceptually but lacks fluency in using the long addition procedure, she might try to remediate that understanding with additional instruction or drills focusing specifically on the carrying operation. She might drop down to simpler problems first, so the student can start with something he already understands. For example, she might break down the big problem above, taking it one column at a time and asking first "what is 7+5?" If the student says "12," then she can point out how this is a simple case of "carrying the 1" when the sum of a column is greater than 9, and explain how that gets handled when the numbers being added have more than one digit: carrying over to the next column, which is the process of moving the extra 10 from the ones column over to add it into the tens column in this case. If, on the other hand, the teacher believes that the student does not understand the place value system conceptually, then she might work on building intuition about the relationship between numbers and their underlying quantities, and the way multi-digit numbers are composed by "bundling up" 10 ones to create a 10, bundling up 10 tens to create 100, and so on, and then relate this conceptually to the reason for carrying the ones in long addition. Note that the teacher's instructional response to the student will be different depending on the data the teacher has about the cause of the student's misconception. This is an example of what is meant by data-driven instruction, or formative assessment.

Example #2: Social Studies

In a social studies class, imagine the assignment is to argue for or against the use of preservatives and other additives in packaged foods, backing up the argument with specific scientific evidence. One student in the class argues

> Companies should not be allowed to use artificial preservatives and other food additives that are synthesized in a laboratory in the packaged foods they produce. Such additives are not natural, according to Webster's (2013) definition of natural, which is "existing in or caused by nature; not made or caused by humankind." Unnatural substances have unknown side effects when ingested into the human body and therefore may be dangerous.

Let's run through the key questions for this case:

What is the key error? The fundamental problem here is that the dictionary definition is cited as evidence, but does not constitute valid evidence of the point being made.

What is the probable reason the student made this error? One possible reason for the error is that the student does not understand the structure of an argument, or what distinguishes it from other writing forms such as narratives. The fragment of her essay, however, suggests that she does seem to understand the basic structure of an argument—she provided a thesis statement (that is, that companies should not be allowed to use artificial food additives) and presented a series of logically connected statements. She also attempted to use evidence to support her argument. The most probable reason for the error, on this analysis, is that the student does not understand what qualifies as scientific evidence.

How can I guide this student to avoid this error in the future? Based on the diagnosis, the teacher might provide feedback to the student about why the dictionary definition does not constitute evidence supporting her thesis. She might also provide a few additional examples of good and bad uses of evidence as models for the student to review and ask her to write a short reflection paper on what the good examples have in common and what differentiates them from the bad examples.

As the examples illustrate, the three questions introduced above provide a general strategy for using formative assessment in a specific situation. In particular these questions prompt us to specify

- A way to detect and define the key error; for example, a measurement instrument (like a test), plus an interpretive framework (like an answer key) to determine when an error has been made and what the specific error is.

- A framework for inferring the probable cause of the error; for example, an inventory of the concepts and skills being learned, with a way to translate the observed error (misspelling the word *ceiling* as *cieling* on a spelling quiz, for example) into a diagnosis of the faulty underlying concept or skill (in this case, the student hasn't mastered the spelling rule "i before e when the sound is long e except after c").

- A set of instructional options for the teacher to use, which are causally linked to the diagnostic error. In the case of the spelling error, for example, the teacher might remind the student of the rule, or have her complete a worksheet (or a game) where she has to apply the rule to identify which words containing ie or ei vowel combinations are spelled correctly and which are spelled incorrectly, in an effort to remediate the faulty spelling knowledge.

In addition to the three questions provided by Elawar and Corno, note that having a way to prioritize teacher time is another factor influencing how effectively teachers can use formative assessment in a classroom setting.

This discussion gives us another way to think about the difference between summative assessment and formative assessment. Summative assessment answers the question, "How did the student perform against a set of benchmarks?" Formative assessment, in contrast, answers questions such as "What misunderstanding caused a student to make a specific error, and what can be done to improve his understanding so he is less likely to make that type of error in the future?"

 A CLOSER LOOK A generation ago, legendary education professor and psychologist Benjamin Bloom was searching for group instruction methods that might be as effective as one-to-one tutoring. Read about it at https://bit.ly/1Sxbgfm.

How Can Classroom Teachers Use Formative Assessment More Effectively?

In an effort to improve the effectiveness of group instruction in a classroom setting, people have developed many different teaching methods such as mastery learning, activity centers, Response to Intervention (RTI), project-based learning, the flipped classroom, special education programs, gifted and talented programs, leveled reading and math groups, and so on. In light of the foregoing discussion, it may or may not surprise you to discover that virtually all such methods can be viewed fundamentally as different strategies for managing and employing the use of formative assessment in the classroom in an effort to produce more effective learning outcomes.

In the next section we examine several different kinds of strategies that leverage formative assessment to increase the effectiveness of group instruction. Before we dive into those methods, however, it is helpful to begin with an overview of the elements of formative assessment itself.

As discussed previously, formative assessment is a *process*, not a product. Specifically, it is a process of using data (measurement) to track student understanding (evaluation), determine the source of any knowledge gaps or misconceptions (diagnosis), and take corrective action (intervention). If the teacher collects data (through either a formal test or an informal observation) but does not use the data to adjust instruction and/or to provide feedback to the student, then there is no formative assessment.

Evaluating Teaching Methods with Respect to Their Use of Formative Assessment

As mentioned previously, many teaching strategies and tactics have been devised in an effort to make group instruction more effective, and most of them can reasonably be understood as attempts to increase the degree to which teachers can use formative assessment effectively in a classroom. It is useful to compare and contrast different teaching methods in this light. The discussion will be facilitated greatly if we first introduce a framework for analyzing different teaching methods that highlights their use of key elements of formative assessment.

As illustrated in Figure 2.1 in the prior chapter, we can productively think of formative assessment as a loop with four key steps: measurement, evaluation, diagnosis, and intervention. In one-on-one instruction, the teacher typically carries out all four of these steps (in a tight loop in close coordination with the student). In theory, though, a student or some other system (such as computer software or a mechanical device) might also perform one or more of these steps. (Note that it is also possible to introduce additional teachers, teaching assistants, parents, and other human resources into the system. For the purposes of this book, we will focus on methods used within a typical classroom where a single teacher works with a group of 20–30 students. The analysis carried out in the text can be extended readily to include additional scenarios.) To facilitate our comparison of different instructional methods, we can use the graphical checklist (or matrix) shown in Figure 3.1. Listed across the top are the four steps of the formative assessment loop, and listed down the left are the options for who or what carries out each step of the process.

As a starting point, consider how we might use this matrix diagram to represent four common instructional design elements (Figures 3.2a–d): one-on-one instruction, classroom lecture (no interaction with students), question-and-answer period following the lecture, and homework exercises.

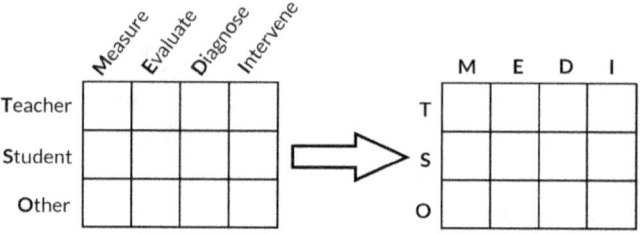

The steps of the formative assessment process are listed along the top, and the people or systems that might carry out a step are listed down the left. The abbreviated version on the right will be used throughout the text.

Figure 3.1. Checklist tool (matrix) for analyzing, comparing, and contrasting different instructional methods in terms of their use of formative assessment.

In one-on-one instruction, as we have discussed, the teacher takes primary responsibility for measuring students' understanding (by observing them as they work problems and asking probing questions, for example), evaluating their understanding, diagnosing any gaps or misconceptions, and intervening (adapting instruction accordingly). This is reflected in the matrix analysis of Figure 3.2a, where the teacher carries out all steps. That has historically been the gold standard of formative assessment and adaptive instruction. One reason is that teachers—by definition—are both the subject matter experts and the instructional experts in the classroom, which makes them the most adept at interpreting student understanding from observable student behavior and responding appropriately to facilitate learning.

Compare one-on-one instruction to a lecture format where there is no interaction between teacher and students (Figure 3.2b). Lecture is a method of broadcasting information from one (teacher) to many (students)—like television. As such, there is no feedback loop from students back to the teacher (at least in the "pure" lecture format) and consequently there can be no adaptation of the instruction. Note that this is not to say that lecture is *bad* or should never be used—quite the contrary. Lecture is a useful instructional design element that can be used very effectively to achieve certain objectives. On its own, however, it does not allow for formative assessment or adaptation of instruction, and so it should not be overused in situations where we have diverse learners and need to help them all achieve a specified set of standards or learning objectives.

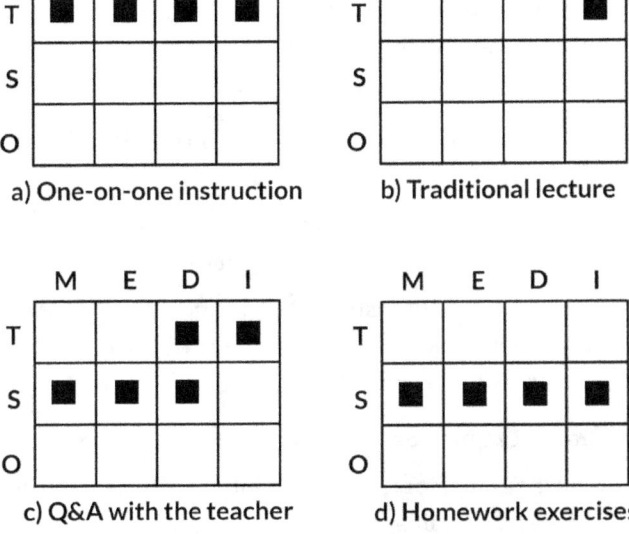

Figure 3.2: Matrix representation of four common instructional design elements

Next, consider a question-and-answer period at the end of a lecture (Figure 3.2c). Students initiate questions based on what they heard in the lecture. Students, therefore, have to reflect on their own state of understanding (internal measurement and evaluation), and then they have to diagnose the root of any knowledge gaps or misconceptions (diagnosis), and then they have to formulate a question that will elicit an answer from the teacher that will help them clarify or refine their understanding. The teacher might probe the questioner to make sure he understands what is being asked and why—that is why both the student and teacher are identified with the "Diagnosis" step in Figure 3.2c. Finally, the teacher provides a response tailored to the student's need (intervention), to the extent the actual need is clear to him at that point. Unlike the lecture itself, this kind of exchange does entail the use of formative assessment. The virtues of this kind of question-and-answer period are that

- It is general (it works for all kinds of content).
- It is low-overhead for the teacher (no special preparation or instructional design required).
- It is of variable duration, which means the duration can be made to fit the available time easily on-the-fly.
- The answer to one student's question can benefit a number of students who might have the same misunderstanding or knowledge gap.

Drawbacks include that

- It pushes much of the responsibility onto the students to measure, evaluate, and diagnose their own state of understanding or misunderstanding (and they might not be very good at that).

- It requires students to formulate a precise question that will help the teacher understand what they need (and they might not be very good at that).
- It inherently prioritizes the needs of the students who are most willing to ask for help, which may not be the students who need it most.
- It addresses student issues one at a time, which runs up against the limits discussed previously on the average amount of time available per student.

PAUSE AND THINK Take a moment to think about other tactics you use in your own teaching and how you would represent them using the formative assessment matrix. For example, do you ever use the Socratic method of questioning in which you pose questions to specific students as a way of tracking their understanding instead of waiting for students to generate their own questions? How would a representation of the Socratic method compare to that of student-driven questions shown in 3.2c?

Finally, consider a set of homework exercises that a teacher might assign to students following a lecture in class (Figure 3.2d). Imagine students are working on their homework alone at home. Maybe they have to conjugate verbs in Latin for homework or complete a set of problems from the back of the book in algebra, or diagram and explain the structure and function of the major components of a cell in biology. Since students are assumed to be working alone, they are responsible for measuring and evaluating their own understanding, diagnosing any gaps or misconceptions, and intervening to adapt the material to facilitate their own learning (such as making flash cards, tracing through their math computation to locate the source of an error and correct it, or rereading a section of the biology textbook). Students differ widely in their ability and motivation to do this—at one end, some students will not even bother trying to do the homework, while at the other end some students will go to great lengths to make the work as excellent as they can and verify that it is correct.

A key virtue of these kinds of exercises is that they are completed in a distributed manner—students work on them in parallel, at their own pace, and teachers can review the set afterwards to identify areas where individual students or the class may need additional attention or depth. Exercises can be a good opportunity for students to use formative assessment on their own, but much depends on the design of the exercise (in particular, whether students can get the feedback they need to adapt instruction themselves) and on the ability and initiative of students to make it work.

SKINNY SKETCH: Designing Effective Formative Assessment Questions

A good formative assessment question is specifically designed to serve two purposes:

1. It reliably distinguishes between students who do and do not understand the target concept or skill, which is what enables the teacher to *evaluate* whether the group is ready to move on to the next topic.

(continues)

(continued)

2. Wrong answers are designed to provide the teacher with *diagnostic insight* about the most important student misconceptions, which is what enables the teacher to determine what specific kind of instructional adaptation is appropriate.

Consider this multiple-choice math example (you'll see it again in Chapter 4). Whichever answer the students pick will tell the teacher something about their understanding of long addition:

```
  567
+ 325
-----
   ?
```

A. 882   **B.** 8812   **C.** 892   **D.** 992

Note that this problem is itself complex enough to probe students' understanding of the concept without being tricky or unnecessarily difficult. In particular, there is only one column (the ones column) that sums to more than 10, generating an extra 1 they have to carry (to the tens column). Let's look at each possible response in turn.

A. 882. Students who choose this answer typically know how to sum the individual columns (they can calculate simple sums) but don't yet understand the procedure for adding arbitrary large numbers together. They may also not understand how the number system encodes numbers—otherwise, they would know better than to simply discard any part of the quantities they are working with when composing a sum. However, they do probably understand that each column (other than the leftmost one) can hold only one number.

(continues)

(continued)

An intervention should further develop their understanding that numbers are quantities, addition is the process of joining quantities, and therefore all the quantities that come up in the process of addition have to be accounted for—nothing can be discarded.

B. 8812. Students who choose this answer may have a somewhat better grasp of how the number system works than those who choose option A, in that they know better than to discard any part of the partial sum from the ones column. They do not understand the mechanics of the long addition process, though, so instead of carrying the 10, they simply wrote down the 12 as two digits in the ones column, and this is where the teacher should focus in the intervention.

C. 892. This is the correct answer. The teacher should keep in mind that some students may have randomly guessed the correct answer.

D. 992. Students who select this answer may understand the basic mechanics of the long addition procedure without understanding the base-10 number system. They seem to have carried the 1 correctly into the tens column but then—not understanding what the numerals or the carrying action actually represent—erroneously continued carrying it to the hundreds column. These students may be performing the calculation by rote, and in an intervention they need to further develop their understanding of the base-10 number system, cementing the conceptual link between the formal addition operation and how it corresponds to the transformation of the underlying quantities.

(continues)

(continued)

As this example illustrates, each of the wrong answers gives the teacher some nuanced insight into the nature of student misconceptions that can inform how she adapts instruction for the particular group of students she is working with at that moment.

The same general design principles hold no matter what the subject matter is. If the target concept were spelling rules (such as "i before e when the sound is long e except after c") or the primary causes of the American Revolutionary War, or the separation of powers in the U.S. government, or Newtonian mechanics in physics, or just about anything else, the teacher could similarly develop questions to probe student understanding about those concepts, using common student misconceptions to generate the erroneous response options and plan appropriate interventions to address them.

In addition to creating your own formative assessment questions as described in the previous section, you may also be able to find or adapt questions available via the World Wide Web. Just be sure these questions are well-designed and will provide the information you need to evaluate and diagnose student understanding and make appropriate adjustments to your instruction.

 A CLOSER LOOK For more discussion and resources on developing your own formative assessment tools, see the work of Susan M. Brookhart, especially her 2010 book, *Formative Assessment Strategies for Every Classroom (ASCD)*.

Key Takeaways

- Prioritizing student learning issues is how we make the most of limited teacher instructional time.

- Allocation of time to different instructional methods is important because learner diversity is always an issue—especially with regard to prior knowledge, learning proficiency, metacognition, and motivation.

- A key variable in choosing instructional methods is how much of the *student learning time* includes high-quality formative assessment.

- Quality control can be challenging, especially when students are left in charge of their own learning.

4

Formative Assessment in Some Group Instruction Scenarios

The adaptive instruction process that we discussed in Chapter 2 works great in a one-on-one teaching scenario, where the teacher can spend all of her time monitoring, evaluating, diagnosing, and adapting instruction for one student the whole time. Add even one more student, and the teacher now has significantly less time to observe, evaluate, diagnose, and adapt instruction for each individual. With a 2:1 ratio, she has to worry about prioritization (which student needs help more and how can she keep track of that?), time allocation (which student to work with when, for how long, and on what?), and the inefficiencies of moving from student to student—that is, time spent "catching up" with the second student. As Figure 4.1 illustrates, the most precipitous drop occurs when adding just one more student.

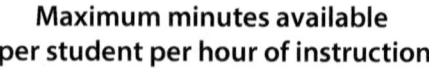
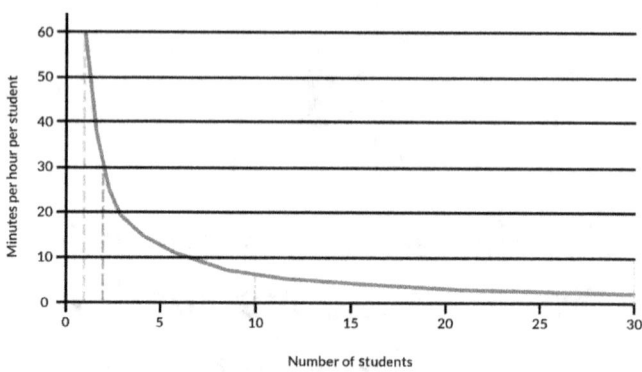

Figure 4.1: The average amount of time a teacher has available to spend with individual students.

Raise the ratio to 30:1, and what's a teacher to do? Is there any way to practice formative assessment in such conditions? The short answer is yes—with the help of technology.

In this chapter we'll consider five ways of bringing more formative assessment into classroom instruction (Figure 4.2). They include

1. "clickers" in an interactive lecture,
2. Internet video in a flipped classroom,
3. a catalog system in programmed instruction,
4. a mobile device with an adaptive curriculum, and
5. the World Wide Web with a teacher dashboard.

Let's take each one in sequence, looking at the particular scenario, how it works, and its benefits and drawbacks.

FORMATIVE ASSESSMENT IN SOME GROUP INSTRUCTION SCENARIOS

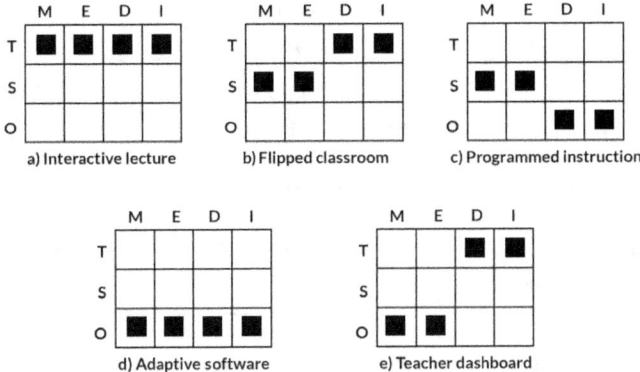

Figure 4.2: Matrix representation of five additional instructional design elements

Interactive Lecture

The Scenario

As Ms. Gray finishes explaining how to "carry the ones" in long addition, she turns away from the sample problem she has just worked through on the whiteboard and looks out at the faces of her students. "Now let's see you try one," she says. The students know the drill—they pick up their clickers and look at the problem that is projected on the screen. It looks like this:

> 567
>
> + 325
>
> ?
>
> **A.** 882
>
> **B.** 8812
>
> **C.** 892
>
> **D.** 992

Students work out the problem on paper, and then select their answer using the four buttons on the clicker. Ms. Gray taps her keyboard to project a graph of their responses on the screen (Figure 4.3).

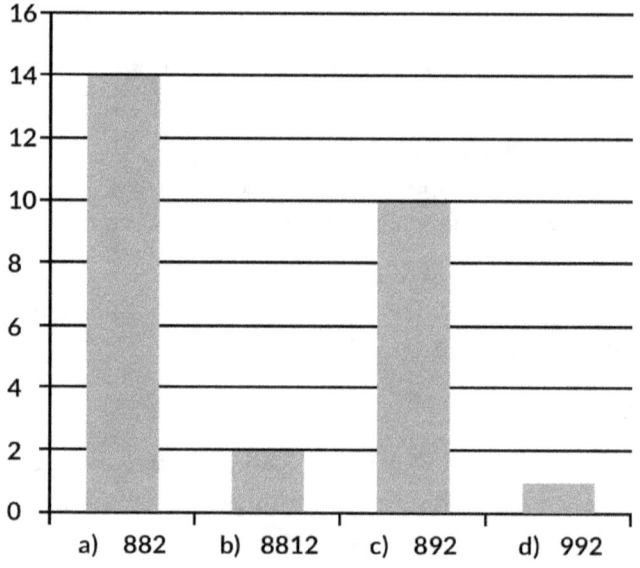

Figure 4.3: Tally of student responses to a multiple-choice math problem

Ms. Gray can see immediately that she needs to spend more time on this topic. Less than half the class chose the correct answer—C) 892. The wrong answers (A, B, and D) are designed to give her clues about the nature of students' misunderstanding. Most students who answered incorrectly chose A) 882. These students simply failed to carry the 1 when they added 7+5 in the ones column. They probably produced the right answer (12), wrote down the 2, and then didn't know what to do with the 10 so they just ignored it and moved on to the next column. The students who answered B) 8812 have a similar problem—they added 7+5, correctly produced 12, and instead of carrying the 10 they wrote down the number 12 (in the ones column) before moving on to the next column.

The good news is that all of these kids can probably add small numbers fine, so Ms. Gray knows she needs to focus specifically on the carrying operation. She decides to have them work through some simpler, more concrete problems with bundles of popsicle sticks to help the students build intuition about what happens with the "extra" 1 in a column, and then she works with them to connect the quantities of popsicle sticks to written equations.

Later she gives the students another long addition problem. This time, most students give the correct answer. Ms. Gray decides that's good enough for the moment—she will spend some time with the stragglers in a small group during their next activity center period—and moves on to start lecturing on the next topic.

How It Works

The interactive lecture (represented in Figure 4.2a) is a hybrid of the standard lecture and one-on-one instruction adapted to work with a group instead of an individual. The basic idea is to introduce concepts through lecture and examples, immediately measure the group's collective understanding of key concepts, and adapt the lecture based on whether the majority of the group (or some other fraction of students) is demonstrating sufficient understanding.

In the simplest adaptation, the teacher has to make two critical decisions:

1. How much time to spend on a given topic, which is determined by how well the students are performing as a group

2. What specific misconceptions or gaps in understanding to prioritize in that time, which is determined by the distribution of wrong answers, and what those wrong answers indicate about the nature of specific student misconceptions

Five key elements of an interactive lecture are

1. **Lecture:** A regular lecture, divided into relatively short chunks (or mini-lectures), where each mini-lecture corresponds to one key idea. The lecture is used to introduce new information to students. The first mini-lecture in the vignette, for example, introduces the procedure for carrying ones in long addition.

2. **Measurement:** Two or more well-designed formative assessment questions per mini-lecture—one for the initial assessment to decide how to adapt and at least one to follow-up and gauge the success of the intervention. (See Chapter 3, "Components of Formative Assessment in Practice," for tips on question design.)

3. **Evaluation strategy:** The teacher needs to decide what overall group performance on the assessment is "good enough" to move on to the next topic versus what is insufficient and requires adaptation. For example, will they move on when at least half of the students can produce the right answer, should they work until at least two-thirds of students demonstrate understanding, or is it acceptable to move on when only a third of students "get it"?

4. **Diagnostic rubric:** A diagnosis of the student misconception associated with each wrong answer in the formative assessment questions.

5. **Adaptive intervention plan:** A plan for how to address each type of misunderstanding diagnosed in the previous step.

Some Potential Benefits

In the interactive lecture, the teacher retains some control over pacing and coverage but has more insight into whether and how students are making sense of the material. If the formative assessment questions are well-designed, she also gleans insights that inform prioritization—that is, how she should adapt the instruction. In this scenario, the teacher's instructional decisions are based on data from *every* student instead of being driven by the needs of the few who are willing to raise their hand and ask a question. It is as though all of the students voted on what the teacher should talk about next, instead of the one student with their hand raised who happens to be called upon that drives that decision for the whole group.

Some Potential Drawbacks

Like any lecture, the interactive lecture is less effective than one-to-one instruction. Students who understand the concept immediately will still have to spend time going over material they already know, while others may still not understand by the time the teacher needs to move on. This method also requires additional preparation and instructional design from the teacher, over and above what would be required to deliver a standard lecture. For example, high-quality formative assessment questions must be developed in advance, and the teacher must be prepared to deviate from a scripted lecture to meet the students' needs with additional lecture or other activities, without necessarily knowing in advance what those specific needs might be. Of course, these materials can also be built up and refined over time.

The Flipped Classroom

The Scenario

When he started out teaching world history, Mr. Green spent most of the time in class lecturing to his students on key historical events covered in the textbook. For homework he then had them review the relevant textbook sections and answer a series of questions about the ideas covered in the lecture and reading. He would also quiz students regularly on historical facts (names, dates, locations, significance, and so on) to gauge how well they were retaining the material.

Last year, Mr. Green "flipped" his classroom. That is, he recorded his standard lectures and made them available to students online. Instead of coming to class to listen to lectures, his students are now required to watch each lecture *before* the class period, and he develops what used to be homework assignments into classroom activities.

Sometimes they play "World History Trivia" in teams, for example, where the categories and questions are based on the historical facts he wants them to learn. Students buzz in for a chance to give their answer. Sometimes they form small groups to discuss the questions at the end of the textbook chapter and then each group shares their thinking with the whole class during a plenary debrief. At other times they debate competing interpretations of historic events, such as reasons for the start of the Civil War or the Great Depression.

How It Works

The flipped classroom (Figure 4.2b) looks like a combination of homework exercises and the gold standard of one-on-one instruction. It provides all of the elements necessary for formative assessment: measurement, evaluation, diagnosis, and intervention. Students work on problems individually or in a group and monitor their own understanding (measurement). If they get stuck, the teacher can intervene either on his own or at the students' request—the teachable moment—and probe further to figure out what the problem is (diagnosis), then take appropriate action to improve student understanding (adaptive intervention).

While swapping what happens in class and what happens at home might seem like a small change to the instructional design, it can have very big consequences. Time spent delivering a prepared lecture is precious instructional time that is not leveraging the teacher's ability to adapt instruction to individual student needs. Moving lectures out of class time frees up a lot of time for the teacher to interact with students, while also leveraging the time the class is all together for engaging in activities they would not be able to do alone—discussion, debate, comparing and contrasting viewpoints, team competition, and so on.

The flipped classroom also enables Mr. Green to collect richer formative assessment data on student understanding than he would get from delivering a lecture, and allows him to respond immediately when teachable moments arise, which is not possible when the exercises are done at home. In the latter case, the student might encounter a conceptual difficulty on the homework on Monday night, turn it in on Tuesday, and then Mr. Green might correct it by Tuesday night. So the earliest he could respond to the student's need is a full two days later! By that time, the student's "teachable moment" has long passed and any adaptive feedback will not be nearly as effective as it would have been in that moment, if it has any effect at all.

The technologies to support lecture recording have become inexpensive and ubiquitous, and teachers can find support from their schools, colleagues, or even students if they need help in this area. One way to make the out-of-school experience more engaging is to provide incentives for students to watch the videos. Some teachers give points for simple completion, which can be monitored by having students complete an assignment that would be easy for anyone who has watched the video. Others require students to complete a more substantive activity after watching the video but before coming to class, such as making a blog post, a discussion post, or a response to someone else's post.

The biggest challenge in the flipped classroom is designing in-class activities that maximize the opportunity of having teachers and students together in an interactive setting. These activities should be designed with formative assessment in mind. Discussions and teamwork can be good because they require students to make their thinking public, which in turn provides formative assessment data to the teacher. Playful competitions become possible and can be very motivating to many students. Students can work problems and be invited to notify the teacher when they need help. The teacher can make note of how individual students are doing and adapt the instruction on-the-fly by adjusting where to allow additional time and understanding what misconceptions or knowledge gaps are common and may warrant an individual or group intervention.

One simple design is to have students work independently at their desks on exercises while the teacher walks the room checking in on students and providing encouragement, feedback, and individualized support. This takes advantage of the fact that the students and teacher are together in the same room by the use of formative assessment and differentiation over the classical model of in-class lectures and homework exercises, but does not leverage the opportunity for peer learning, feedback, and support. Having students playfully compete or work in groups can provide more opportunities for engaging students, making learning visible (for measurement, evaluation, and diagnosis), and distributing part of the responsibility for adapting instruction in real-time to the students, potentially increasing the opportunities for effective use of formative assessment. In these cases, the teacher may have to think more carefully about how to assess individual student progress and needs in the context of the group work.

Some Potential Benefits

The flipped classroom can free up substantial amounts of teacher time to diagnose student needs using formative assessment and adapt instruction accordingly. Exercises are very useful for helping students internalize target knowledge, but students vary in their ability to evaluate their own knowledge, diagnose misconceptions and knowledge gaps, and figure out how to repair them. Moving exercises into class time where the students have access both to teachers and peers while working through problems increases the chances that they can get the support they need and get the most out of those learning experiences.

Teachers can acquire much richer formative assessment data on student understanding with the flipped classroom than they could get under the traditional model. Teachers can even choose to incorporate some of the data-collection strategies and tools described in the interactive lecture. For example, in a modified game of World History Trivia, the teacher could use formative assessment software to have all students "buzz in," which will determine not only which student responded first for purposes of awarding points but simultaneously collect formative data from all students that can inform adaptive instruction.

For students, watching recorded lectures can enable them to control their own pacing in receiving the content—that is, to watch and rewind as often as they like. If they miss a class, they can still view the lecture. If they do not understand a point being made, they have a whole Internet full of resources they can use to supplement the main lecture. (Teachers might offer some suggestions in order to maintain quality control.)

Some Potential Drawbacks

For some teachers, the idea of recording lectures in advance of class may be an obstacle. For one thing, this may require more planning and preparation than delivering a live lecture. In some subject areas, the subject matter does not change very rapidly and so lecture videos can be used for many years without change. In other subject areas, the subject matter may change more frequently, requiring the teacher to invest more time in editing and rerecording videos on an ongoing basis.

At the same time, teachers will need to invest the time to develop a new set of learning activities for each class period that are creative, engaging, and effective and that leverage formative assessment and support more differentiated instruction. This could represent a more substantial investment of time and energy than preparing a set of homework assignments does in the traditional classroom.

Also, when students are required to watch lectures on their own outside of class, less self-regulated or self-motivated learners might skip lectures, leaving them unprepared to participate in class activities—although note that this problem already exists with students who skip homework, and watching videos on their own is less challenging than doing exercises on their own.

Students can work at their own pace within a single class period, but all students are brought back to the same starting point with each video lecture and associated exercises, which means this strategy provides a limited amount of individualization with respect to pacing through the curriculum overall.

Lastly, flipped classrooms also require that students have access to a computer with reliable Internet connectivity outside of school so they can watch the videos before class. Teachers should not assume all students do.

Programmed Instruction

The Scenario

Ms. Black announces to her fourth-grade students that it's time for individual reading activities. Each student reads their assigned passage and answers a series of questions probing vocabulary, grammar, comprehension, and other core reading skills. Students record their answers in the workbook. They then check their own work with an answer key and review explanations of the problems so they can correct any errors or misconceptions. Ms. Black walks the room to make sure students are all engaged and progressing, elaborates on explanations in the answer key, answers questions and remediates misconceptions, and provides encouragement.

At the end of the week, Ms. Black reviews each student's charted progress with them and they determine together whether the student should continue at the same level the following week, advance to the next level, or perhaps move back down a level for a bit more practice. The teacher also uses these formative data to identify any concepts or skill areas that might need particular attention and adapts instruction as appropriate for individual students, small groups, or the whole class.

How It Works

Ms. Black is employing a method of instruction called *Programmed Instruction* (Figure 4.2c) that breaks down a curriculum into a logical sequence of small instructional steps covering increasingly complex concepts and skills. After each step, the student is required to make an active response that tests their understanding of the instruction in that step, possibly also building on any or all preceding steps. The student typically must demonstrate understanding of a concept or skill before moving on (an example of *mastery learning*), and there are multiple activities at the same level so he can keep working on fresh content until he masters it.

All of the steps of formative assessment are covered: measurement, evaluation, diagnosis, and intervention.

The interesting difference here is that the bulk of the formative assessment and adjustment is carried out by students themselves as they follow the program. Making formative assessment a student responsibility frees them up to work at their own pace. It also allows teachers to operate at a higher level—addressing unexpected issues, working individually with students when they need it, looking for patterns of misconceptions that might call for adapting other parts of the instruction, and so on. In this model, diagnosis and intervention are embodied in the curriculum and the materials themselves.

To complete the formative assessment loop, the students follow the instructions to generate answers to some questions or problems (this is the *measurement*). Then they check their own work by comparing their answers to the answer key (*evaluation*). In some curricula, the answer key (or some supplementary material) also includes explanations for why the right answer is right and what makes the wrong answers wrong. This is where the program designers can embed the *diagnosis* step in the curriculum itself—if they can anticipate the most likely student misconceptions and craft wrong answer options that students holding each misconception will select. The student's pattern of right and wrong answers represents a diagnosis of which conceptions are correct and which are incorrect (and in what way).

The final step, adapting the *intervention*, occurs in two ways. First, feedback must be differentiated to help remediate particular student misconceptions based on their specific pattern of errors. Second, it must be adapted by individualized pacing, which keeps each student at the same level of challenge for as long as they need to demonstrate consistent understanding and mastery at that level before moving up. The system also handles this by defining criteria for moving up, moving down, or staying at the same level. As the vignette with Ms. Black illustrates, a teacher might adjust those criteria alone or in conversation with the student, which is a great way to invite students deeper into the learning process and give them more ownership of their own learning.

How It Works

The easiest way to use Programmed Instruction in the classroom is to use a pre-packaged curriculum, such as the classic SRA Reading Laboratory, still available today from McGraw-Hill. Teachers administer a pretest to identify initial placement level. Students are then given materials and begin work at their own pace, asking the teacher for help if they get stuck. Ideally, teachers review student progress regularly (either with the student or not) in order to develop detailed insight into each student's academic development, as well as to identify additional adaptations they might make to the instruction for individual students, small groups, or the whole class.

Some Potential Benefits

Because Programmed Instruction offloads some of the diagnosis and adaptive intervention steps from the teacher, it has the potential to be much more scalable than methods that rely completely on the teacher to diagnose and adapt in real time for several students. This method also supports the efficient use of time and resources; students are working at their own pace and so are neither held back unnecessarily nor pushed forward before they are ready as they are in some methods (such as traditional lectures). Teachers can prioritize where their instructional time can be most usefully invested, perhaps allowing them to handle higher-order, more complex instruction.

Students must demonstrate mastery, which in itself supports differentiation and accommodation of different student capabilities and needs, at least with respect to pacing and allocation of time, and often in terms of differentiated feedback in response to a pattern of errors (although this depends, of course, on how well the subject matter lends itself to doing this and how capable the instructional designers are at designing it effectively).

Some Potential Drawbacks

Programmed Instruction works best for a certain kind of subject matter, activity, and learning outcome—in particular, it works best when instructional designers can split the curriculum into a series of activities following a well-defined progression of difficulty. Math and basic reading skills are two examples. The approach works less well for developing higher order competencies like analyzing a text where multiple valid interpretations might be possible, or for creative productions like writing an essay on a general theme or producing a piece of art. By narrowing the type of activity that can be employed, programmed instruction may narrow the range of pathways that students can follow to reach mastery compared to some other methods. Also the fact that students manage their own learning can be a challenge for those who do not like the format and/or have weaknesses in this area (ranging from low achievement motivation to a clinical condition such as ADHD or executive function disorder).

Adaptive Educational Software

The Scenario

Mrs. Weller directs her first-grade students to the iPad cart and asks each of them to take a device back to their seat to continue work on the adaptive math curriculum that they have been using. The students know what to do: they pick up a device, launch the app, and select their name from within the student roster that pops up. The app takes them to a screen showing their progress and achievements to date and the activity they were working on last time. The student taps the icon for that activity and gets to work. The app models what the student is meant to do in each type of activity and then presents a series of tasks for the student to complete. It also measures the student's performance (for example, tracking correct or incorrect responses, as well as speed of response as a measure of fluency), and adapts the instruction accordingly. If a student appears to be stuck or flailing, the app might provide a bit of context-sensitive direct instruction or a hint specific to the concept or skill that is giving her trouble. If the student struggles too much for too long, the app will drop her down a level. If, on the other hand, a student gets a series of tasks correct quickly, the app will rapidly move her up to a more challenging level of activity and perhaps introduce a new concept or skill for her to work on. In this way, the adaptive curriculum keeps most students working at their "just right" level most of the time.

The app is mastery-based, which means students do not move on to a new activity until they have demonstrated understanding and fluency with the concepts covered in the current activity. Consequently, the amount of time spent on a concept or skill will vary widely across students, depending on what they need to do to achieve the standard of mastery on that topic. One student who has already learned a concept at home may spend five minutes demonstrating their fluency, while another student who is just encountering the concept for the first time might spend many hours reaching the same level of mastery.

While students are engaged in this way, Mrs. Weller is free to pull aside a small group of five students who, based on a review of their progress in the app, appear to be struggling with basic number concepts. She can work with them directly using hands-on math manipulatives to help build their intuition about these important foundational concepts. After a period of 15 minutes, she sends these students back to their desks to work and calls over another small group of students who have difficulty ordering numbers by magnitude.

How It Works

Adaptive educational software (represented in Figure 4.2d) takes the form of a computer program (on desktops, mobile devices, or tablets) that uses formative assessment to adjust instruction for each student based on their past performance. To be truly adaptive, a software application must perform all of the steps of formative assessment: it must *measure* student performance, *evaluate* the quality of that performance against some meaningful standard, *diagnose* what the student needs if he or she has not met the standard, and *intervene* adaptively based on that diagnosis. It must adjust the instruction, feedback, task difficulty, pacing, and so on based on the student performance.

If the student has demonstrated understanding, the software should move him on quickly; if the student has not demonstrated sufficient understanding, it should keep him working where he is, or move him down to a simpler level, as appropriate. Many providers claim their software is adaptive. The litmus test is whether the software can successfully execute the whole formative assessment process to keep most students working at their "just right" level reliably.

The first step is to identify software that fits your purpose. It should be appropriate in terms of scope (for example, covering math facts, math operations, or problem solving, depending on your learning objectives), level (for instance, introducing concepts, increasing fluency, or developing strategic problem solving skills), and instructional design (for example, employing evidence-based best practices for effective learning design).

Identifying and selecting apps is more challenging than it might appear. At the time of this writing, Apple alone offers more than 80,000 education products in its app store. Many of these apps are not actually educational, and neither popularity nor price guarantee educational quality or efficacy. Some apps in the educational category are not even instructional—such as those that are considered "creativity" apps or "productivity" apps. These types of apps are different from instructional apps that are explicitly designed to develop specific knowledge and skills.

Not all educational software is adaptive. An app that has each student work through the same fixed number and sequence of problems in the same fixed order is not adaptive. Neither is an app that lets students pick what activity to work on from a menu, gives them a fixed number of problems in that activity, and then returns them to the menu to decide what to do next.

Research has documented key features of effective instructional design that one can use to evaluate instructional apps (see the sidebar "A Closer Look"). A number of these effective design features are directly related to the way an app supports or does not support formative assessment. For example:

- App providers should state the learning objectives explicitly and clearly.

- Students should have to respond frequently in ways that require them to use the knowledge they are learning—not just passively watch videos or read text.

- The app should use data on student performance to adapt the level of challenge to meet the student's current capabilities. This is the heart of formative assessment. .

- Students should work on a concept or skill until they have mastered it and then (and only then) move on to other topics. Mastery learning is only possible when formative assessment is employed

 A CLOSER LOOK For a discussion of evidence-based instructional design features that have been found to support effective learning, check out https://bit.ly/2LVDf1h.

You can incorporate adaptive software into classroom instruction in a number of different ways, including whole class instruction, activity centers, or individual remediation or enrichment. For example, if every student has access to a mobile device in class then the teacher can potentially use the software to deliver one-on-one instruction to the whole class at the same time. Students work on the curriculum and teachers spend their time observing student progress and providing additional support to those who need it most—from simply answering questions and providing encouragement to working more closely with individuals or small groups who might be lagging behind the rest of the group and could benefit from more intensive individualized instruction than that provided by the app.

One common trap teachers should avoid is treating the technology in an "all or none" fashion—that is, acting as if the technology must automatically handle all of the instruction in a subject area for all children or it is considered a failure and not used at all. Teaching is hard work and a high level of skill is required to do it well. Technology is not magic. The iPad by itself is not going to transform education any more than the chalkboard by itself did. Both are powerful tools that can support profound changes in instruction, learning, classroom dynamics, and student outcomes—but only when a teacher incorporates them skillfully into the instructional process.

The critical question to ask about an adaptive technology, in other words, is not, "Does it teach the subject matter effectively?" but instead, "Can it be used to enable the teacher to teach and/or the student to learn the subject matter more effectively than was possible without it?" The standard of success is actual incremental improvement in teacher effectiveness and student outcomes, not idealized perfection. Teachers should think about how any given technology might be used to provide remediation for an individual student who needs additional support, to provide enrichment for students who have mastered the primary curriculum, to provide an engaging and productive "activity center" that students can work on independently, or to support whole class learning in a way that reduces the classroom management burden on the teacher and expands opportunities for the teacher to use formative assessment to provide individualized instruction. If the technology enables teachers and students to perform better in some important way compared to the available alternatives, then that technology is successful, even if it is not perfect in every respect.

Some Potential Benefits

Because all four elements of formative assessment—measurement, evaluation, diagnosis and intervention—are handled by the adaptive software, the technology supports the primary formative assessment loop for all students. It is as if each student has a full-time virtual teaching assistant working one-on-one with him or her to adapt the instruction. For this reason, adaptive software has perhaps the greatest potential for bringing more formative assessment into the classroom and leveraging it to differentiate instruction more effectively.

Students can focus on solving problems by applying the new knowledge they are learning, with less dependence on their ability to follow the protocol of finding the solution to each problem, carefully grading their own work, recording the results, and making choices about where to go next. Well-designed adaptive software will also support students who might have difficulty staying engaged or managing their own learning, so students can focus on learning a set of target concepts and skills with the least disruption or "friction" possible.

Teachers can spend less time supervising these parts of the process and more time working with individual students on developing knowledge, skill, and understanding. Note that this does not imply the technology is able to, or even intended to, replace the teacher. Ideally, the technology can take over some of the lower-level instruction to reduce student behavioral issues and classroom management burden on the teacher, while simultaneously freeing up significant amounts of the teacher's time to focus on differentiating instruction around the more complex learning challenges encountered by students. Teachers are generally in the best position to determine how to use a technology effectively in their own classroom given their particular learning objectives, resources, and constraints.

Some Potential Drawbacks

Using adaptive software in the classroom requires the necessary technology. There may also be special preparation required, since teachers and students often need to install the software and/or create accounts in order to make use of it, and this in turn may require authorization from administrators and help from the technology staff.

As discussed above, identifying appropriate apps can be a challenge for teachers, too. There is a bewildering array of educational applications available today, and these apps vary widely in their design, pedagogy, scope, cost, usability, feasibility for classroom use, alignment with school curriculum, engagement, and effectiveness. It is difficult to discern whether a particular app is usable and effective for learning without actually using it or getting a strong recommendation from another teacher who has used it.

As with programmed instruction, adaptive software currently works well for the kinds of subject matter and learning activities where learning objectives can be defined explicitly and student productions can be evaluated automatically by a computer—it works well for learning spelling, vocabulary, and grammar in language arts, for example, and less well for evaluating the quality of an essay and providing individualized feedback on how to improve the writing (although great progress has been made even in the area of computer scoring of essays, which makes it conceivable that this will become more common in the near future).

Teacher Dashboard

The Scenario

As part of his English language arts curriculum, Mr. Graves has students read books in a digital format online. At the end of each chapter, students complete a series of online activities that simultaneously support their learning and measure their progress. These activities cover a variety of language competencies, including comprehension, vocabulary, inference, grammar, and narrative structure. Students' responses are captured, evaluated, and stored in a database.

At any time, Mr. Graves can launch a dashboard that shows him how much work students have completed to date, what they are working on right now, and how proficient they are in each of the key areas of knowledge and skill. Mr. Graves uses the insights gleaned from the dashboard to inform how he uses class time, homework, projects, and activity centers to help ensure every student meets the district standards in language arts.

How It Works

Digital dashboards tied to computer-based assignments and assessments (Figure 4.2e) enable teachers to get an updated, at-a-glance summary of key measures of progress in a subject area for a group (often a whole class) of students. In the sample dashboard shown in Figure 4.4, student names are listed down the left side, while specific concepts and skills in the curriculum are laid out across the top. In this example, colored shapes in each cell indicate a student's proficiency with each concept or skill, as well as their progress through the curriculum as a whole. At a glance, the teacher can see who is racing ahead, who is straggling, and what concept or skill each student is working on currently.

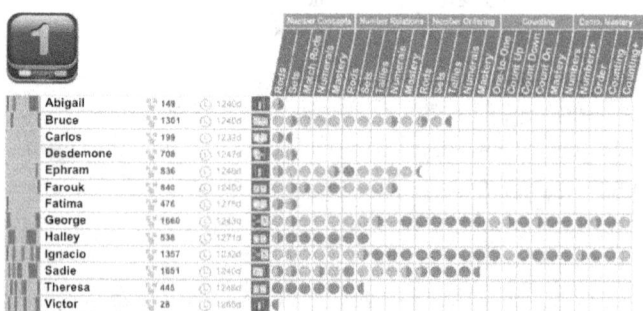

Figure 4.4: A dashboard for tracking student progress in elementary math

In its simplest form, the teacher dashboard provides something like a teacher grade book that is updated in real time as assignments or activities are completed. In terms of the formative assessment process, the *measurement* is done when the student completes an activity on the computer. The *evaluation* is often done by the computer as well—by automatically scoring the student's responses to, say, reading comprehension questions or answers to math problems. The data are then sent to the dashboard where teachers can use them to diagnose and adapt the instructional interventions more easily than they could without technology.

As with adaptive software, the first step is to identify a dashboard platform that works for you given your learning objectives, resources, and constraints. Keep in mind that there will be two major components to consider: 1) what assignments, activities, quizzes, tests, and other materials you will use to track student progress digitally (that's measurement), and 2) the teacher dashboard where the teacher can access and view these data. Typically, the answer to one question determines the answer to the other.

For example, some formative assessment platforms, such as Quizlet (www.quizlet.com), Gradeable (www.gradeable.com), and Socrative (www.socrative.com) allow teachers to create their own formative assessments for any subject and then display the results on a dashboard for tracking student progress. Such platforms also sometimes enable third parties—whether major publishers or other teachers—to provide compatible content for specific subject areas. This is obviously the most flexible option but requires more work from the teacher to create or curate all of the subject area materials, and such content may vary in quality and appropriateness.

At the other end of the spectrum are teacher dashboards that work with specific curricula, such as the teacher dashboard available for the Native Brain[1] math curriculum shown in Figure 4.4 (www.nativebrain.com). When you are choosing curricula or educational apps for classroom use, check whether this kind of dashboard is available. While these dashboards tend to be more limited in terms of the scope of subject matter they can be used with, in these cases the content is already prepared for the teacher and the formative measures (tasks, activities, quizzes, tests, and so on) can be more tightly integrated into the dashboard reporting to further enhance the teacher's ability to adapt the instruction effectively based on student performance.

Some Potential Benefits

Faster updating of student performance data means teachers can respond to teachable moments in real time, as well as have more complete data for planning day to day. Automatic scoring and recording of assignments can save substantial teacher time, which can instead be used for planning and adapting curriculum, and spending time with individual students. In addition, having a summary at-a-glance view of the whole class enables teachers to prioritize how to spend their instructional time most effectively. Students receive more immediate feedback, which is motivating, and the dramatic reduction of the delay between submission and feedback means students are more likely to absorb corrective or reinforcing feedback.

---

[1] Full disclosure: the author is a co-founder of Native Brain, Inc. and a co-creator of its math curriculum and teacher dashboard.

Some Potential Drawbacks

For real-time updates to the teacher dashboard, the student activities and assignments must be designed to work with the particular dashboard that is being used. In some cases—especially if teachers are using curriculum materials designed by a third party instead of creating their own—this means the dashboard and the curriculum (or parts of the curriculum) must be taken as a bundle; it is often not possible to select a dashboard from one provider and the curriculum from another. In these cases, teachers either may be limited to the curricular materials provided with the platform, or if they want to supplement with other materials, might have to manage more than one dashboard for different parts of the curriculum. While not ideal, this might still be workable and useful for the purposes of improving student outcomes by bringing more formative assessment into classroom practice.

Summary

The five instructional strategies reviewed in this chapter share two important features. First, as the analysis makes clear, each of them is designed to make more effective use of formative assessment and differentiate instruction in an effort to meet the diverse capabilities and needs of students in a typical classroom. In that way, they support more effective group instruction (along the lines of the gold standard of one-on-one instruction).

Second, each method is made possible (or at least much more feasible and effective) by at least one technological innovation. The interactive lecture, for example, depends on technology that allows student responses to formative assessment questions to be tallied instantly so the teacher does not have to stop the lecture periodically to manually tally their responses. The flipped classroom depends on student access to instructional videos outside of class—enabled by the World Wide Web plus free video hosting services like YouTube. Programmed instruction was made possible by the invention of the "curriculum lab"—the organization of a curriculum for reading, math, or another subject around sets of carefully leveled activities that students could complete and score on their own, plus the guidelines for moving between levels. Adaptive software is made possible by the availability of classroom computers, and is made even more effective with the advent of mobile technology and one-to-one technology in the classroom. Teacher dashboards are made possible by networking technology—most commonly, the ubiquitous availability of the Internet. The unique affordances of each innovation enable teachers to carry out the formative assessment process with a group of students in a different way (as Figure 4.2 illustrated).

These instructional methods are not mutually exclusive options but rather design elements teachers can combine or pull apart as befits their situation. For example, combining an interactive lecture with adaptive software covering the same subject matter can replace traditional lecture plus exercises in a way that is more engaging to students, more supportive of expert teaching, more differentiated, and more effective. Alternatively, the flipped classroom can be combined with a dashboard to track student progress and present it for teachers to be able to monitor, prioritize, and intervene during class more effectively.

Perhaps the ultimate combination in terms of individualizing instruction and maximizing the use of limited teaching time is a combination of adaptive software plus an integrated teacher dashboard. This allows students to move at their own pace through the entire curriculum (not just per class period as is the case with the flipped classroom) and allows teachers to rapidly identify, prioritize, and intervene immediately when teachable moments arise for individual students.

The best design for a particular teacher will depend on their combination of available technology and resources, curriculum, subject matter, student capabilities and needs, and teacher comfort with the different options. Some experimentation will probably be useful, and other teachers are a great resource for learning about strategies and technologies that have worked in a real classroom setting.

Key Takeaways

- Using formative assessment to adapt instruction always involves four elements: measurement, evaluation, diagnosis, and intervention.
- Skilled teachers know how to use formative assessment in a one-on-one scenario to adapt instruction to an individual learner's capabilities and needs.
- Unfortunately, the tactics that work so well one-on-one quickly fall apart in group instruction.
- Teachers can leverage formative assessment more effectively for group teaching through a combination of systematic instructional design and the use of technology (such as "clickers," online video, mobile apps, and web dashboards).

5

Closing Thoughts

If you take just one idea from this book let it be this: formative assessment is perhaps the most powerful tool available for increasing student achievement and reducing achievement gaps in a classroom setting. Keep in mind that formative assessment is a type of *instructional process*, not a special type of *test*. In particular, formative assessment is the process of using data on student performance to adapt and differentiate instruction to better match individual students' capabilities and needs in order to support higher achievement.

Despite the obscure name, formative assessment is not something new or exotic; it is and always has been the very heart of excellent teaching. It is, in fact, what skilled teachers naturally do when instructing students one-on-one.

The challenge is that the highly individualized teaching methods that work so well one-on-one simply do not work with a group. They start to break down as soon as a second student enters the scene, and their effectiveness continues to degrade very rapidly as the number of students in the group grows.

Taken to an extreme, with a large number of students and no explicit strategy or support for using formative assessment in a group, we end up with the common lecture as the primary teaching method. The pure lecture is a method of broadcasting information to many students, with zero opportunity for formative assessment and therefore zero opportunity for instructional adaptation. The only use of formative assessment in a typical lecture is the tiny amount that can happen during the brief question-and-answer period after the lecture itself is over.

Viewed historically, the heavy reliance on lecture made sense. Opportunities to use formative assessment in the classroom were largely limited by the amount of time teachers could spend individually with each student, which was small in the absence of some kind of supporting technology. The emergence of new technologies like the Internet and mobile computers has changed the game, creating new ways to integrate formative assessment effectively into group instruction, even with a large group. Today there is plenty of evidence that formative assessment can be used in a group setting to produce large gains in student achievement. The key question, then, is how to make it work for all teachers and students.

In prior chapters, we saw that diverse teaching methods can all be viewed fundamentally as different strategies for using formative assessment more effectively at the group level. All of these methods involve *measurement, evaluation, diagnosis,* and *adaptation* of the intervention to meet student capabilities and needs. They differ chiefly in the technology required to make them work, the size of the group used to determine the adaptation, and the frequency of measurement. They also differ based on the rapidity of adapting the intervention, and the ways in which the responsibilities for measurement, evaluation, diagnosis, and intervention adaptation are centralized with the teacher or distributed across students, computers, or other systems (such as the programmed instruction "learning lab" and the adaptive iPad curriculum).

Teachers should not think of these methods as mutually exclusive alternatives where one is strictly better than another—there will be no single "best" approach in all cases. Nor is this meant to represent an exhaustive list of teaching methods by any stretch of the imagination. Instead, we should more properly think of the methods discussed in this book—including familiar methods such as the lecture—as a representative set of design tools that we can combine systematically based on our goals, constraints, and resources in order to achieve the best possible outcome for students. We are then bringing formative assessment more into the center of our instructional practice.

In fact, one might argue that the difference between teacher-centered and student-centered instruction is the degree to which formative assessment is used effectively to differentiate and adapt instruction to the unique capabilities and needs of each student. Bring formative assessment more fully into your classroom practice and you will help every learner achieve closer to their full potential.

Let's Connect!

A book is often like a traditional lecture—a one-way broadcast of information from the author to the readers. It doesn't have to be that way—with social media and other forms of digital communication, this book can be the first exchange in an ongoing dialogue where we can learn from each other.

You can help me by providing formative assessment feedback to inform my writing and teaching. In particular, I would love to hear from you about your experience as you work to apply the ideas and tools presented in this book. It is always wonderful to hear anecdotes and stories illustrating ways you have been successful, and I can use them to refine the presentation of ideas, as well as to inform and inspire others. If, on the other hand, you send a question when you encounter something that isn't clear or you hit a roadblock, not only will you help me understand where I might productively refine the presentation of ideas, but perhaps I or others can help you adapt the tools to be more useful in your particular situation.

Don't forget to visit https://castpublishing.org/skinny-books/using-formative-assessment/resources for links to additional information and resources.

You can reach me on Twitter (@MichaelWConnell), by email at contact@michaelconnell.com, or through www.michaelconnell.com. I wish you all the best and look forward to connecting with you!

References

Black, P., & Wiliam, D. (1998). Assessment and classroom learning. *Assessment in Education: Principles, Policy & Practice, 5*(1), 7–74.

Bloom, B. S. (1984). The 2 Sigma problem: The search for methods of group instruction as effective as one-to-one tutoring. *Educational Researcher, 13*(6), 4–16. Retrieved from http://web.mit.edu/5.95/readings/bloom-two-sigma.pdf.

Brookhart, S. M. (2010). *Formative Assessment Strategies for Every Classroom: An ASCD Action Tool (2nd ed.)*. Alexandria, VA: Association for Supervision and Curriculum. Development.

Elawar, M., & Corno, L. (1985). A factorial experiment in teacher's written feedback on student homework. *Journal of Educational Psychology, 77*(2), 162–173.

Sadler, D. R. (1998). Formative assessment: Revisiting the territory. *Assessment in Education, 5*(1), 77–84.

Sadler, D. R. (1989). Formative assessment and the design of instructional systems. *Instructional Science, 18*(2), 119–144.

CAST Skinny Books®

"Don't tell me everything. Just give me the skinny!"™

Skinny Books by CAST address critical topics of education practice through brief, informative publications that emphasize practical tips and strategies. We talk about these books as "multivitamins"—densely packed with helpful knowledge in a small, digestible format.

Previous books address how to use the iPad for instruction, UDL and the visual arts classroom, and implementing UDL in higher education.

We welcome new proposals. Got an idea? Let us know at *publishing@cast.org*.

You can also purchase this or many other titles on UDL from *www.castpublishing.org*.

www.ingramcontent.com/pod-product-compliance
Lightning Source LLC
Chambersburg PA
CBHW052116110526
44592CB00013B/1628